TENEBRAE

Service of Shadows

Edited by
Lawrence M. Rutherford

Cover art: Crucifixion detail by
Diego de Silva Velazquez (1599-1660)

Cover Design: Lawrence M. Rutherford

Aquinas and More Publishing
Ft. Collins, Colorado

Tenebrae

Service of Shadows

Lawrence M. Rutherford

Copyright © 2017

ISBN-13: 978-0983758198
ISBN-10:0983758190

Copyrights

The Revised Grail Psalms Copyright © 2010, Conception Abbey/The Grail, admin. by GIA Publications, Inc., www.giamusic.com All rights reserved.

New Revised Standard Version Catholic Edition (NRSVCE)
Canticle of Hezekiah (Isaiah 38:10-20) and Canticle of Zechariah (Luke 1:68-79)

Scores accompanying Gospel passages copyright Denis Dobrinski
Used with Permission

All other texts unless noted otherwise © Lawrence M. Rutherford
No part of this work may be reproduced or transmitted in any form or by any means, electronic or mechanical, including photocopying, recording, or by any other information storage retrieval system, without permission in writing from the copyright owner.

PRINTED AND PUBLISHED IN IN THE UNITED STATES OF AMERICA
AQUINAS AND MORE PUBLISHING COMPANY, FT. COLLINS, COLORADO

TENEBRAE

The name Tenebrae is the Latin word for "darkness" or "shadows," and has for centuries been applied to the ancient monastic night and early morning services of the last three days of Holy Week, which in medieval times came to be celebrated on the preceding evenings.

The Psalms and Lamentations are sung using psalm tones similar to the chant heard throughout the day in a monastery.

This service is marked by chanting of Psalms, singing of gospel excerpts, a reading from the *Book of Lamentations* and the gradual extinguishing of candles and other lights until a single candle, a symbol of the Lord, remains.

Towards the end of the service, this candle is hidden, typifying the apparent victory of the forces of evil. At the very end, a loud noise is made, symbolizing the convulsion of nature which followed the death of Jesus Christ. The hidden candle is then restored to its place and by its light all depart in silence.

Alternating men/women or people left/right in the congregation are encouraged to sing the Psalms and canticles with the choir.

*Please stand and
make the Sign of the Cross*

> **P.** Lord, open my lips.
>
> **R. And my mouth will proclaim your praise.**
>
> **P.** Glory to the Father and to the Son, and to the Holy Spirit:
>
> (Bow)
>
> **R. As it was in the beginning, is now, and will be for ever. Amen**

Please sit for the psalmody

1

Psalm 69:1-23

Save me	Ó God,	for the wáters, have rísen	tó my-- neck.
I have súnk into the múd of	*thé deep,*	*where there is*	*nó foot-- - hold.*
I have éntered the waters of	thé deep,	where the flood ov -	er whélms-- me.
I am wéaried with crying aloud; | my throat	*ís parched.*	*My eyes are wásted away with waiting*	*fór my-- God.*
More númerous than the háirs on	mý head	are thóse who háte me	with - out-- cause.
Many are those who attáck me, | enemies	*wíth lies.*	*What I have never stólen, how*	*can Í re - store?*
O God, you knów my	fól - ly;	from you my síns are	nót hid-- - den.
May thóse who hope in you not		*may thóse who seek you not*	
be shamed because of mé, O LORD	*óf hosts;*	*be put to sháme because of me, | O Gód*	*of Ís - ra- el.*
It is for yóu that I suf -	fér taunts,	that sháme has co -	véred my-- face.
To my own kín I have become an	*óut - cast,*	*a stránger to the chíldren*	*of mý mo - ther.*
Zéal for your hóuse con -	súmes me,	and taunts agáinst	you fáll on me.
When my soul wept bítterly in	*fást - ing,*	*they made it a táunt*	*a - gáinst-- me.*
When I máde my clothing sáckcloth I became a repróach	tó them,	the góssip of those at the gátes, the theme	of drúnk – ards songs.
But I práy to you,	*Ó LORD,*	*for a time of*	*your fá -- - vor.*
In your great mércy, answer me,	Ó God,	with your salvátion	that név – er fails.
Réscue me from sínking in	*thé mud;*	*from those who háte me,*	*de -lí – ver me.*
Save me from the wáters of	thé deep,	lest the waves ov -	er whelm -- me.
Let nót the deep en -	*gúlf me,*	*nor the pít close*	*its móuth on me*
LORD, ánswer, for your mércy	ís kind;	in your gréat compássion, turn	to – wárds -- me.
Do not híde your fáce from your	*sér - vant;*	*answer me quíckly, for I*	*am ín dis - tress.*
Come clóse to my sóul and re -	déem me;	ránsom me because	of mý -- foes.
You know my táunts, my sháme, my dis -	hó - nor;	my oppréssors are all	be – fóre-- you.
Taunts have bróken my héart; | here I am in	án - guish.	I looked for sólace, but there was nóne; | for consólers—not	one cóuld I find.
For fóod they gave	*mé gall;*	*in my thírst they gave me vín -*	*e -gar to drink.*

2

I

In Gregorian style

♩=170

Denis Drobinski

Choir

When it was eve' - ning,___ Je _____ sus and the twelve

6

sat down to eat. And Jes - us said _____ un – to them: "One who dips his

Solo

12

bread in this dish with me shall _____ be -

17

Choir

Men

tray me." And each man in turn re - plied: Teach – er is it I?

22

Choir

Men

Teach- er is it I? And to Ju das he re - plied "So you say."

The first candle is extinguished

Psalm 70

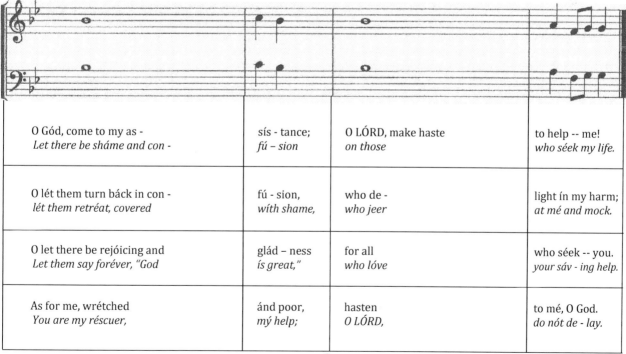

O Gód, come to my as - *Let there be sháme and con -*	sís - tance; *fú – sion*	O LÓRD, make haste *on those*	to help -- me! *who séek my life.*
O lét them turn báck in con - *lét them retréat, covered*	fú - sion, *wíth shame,*	who de - *who jeer*	light ín my harm; *at mé and mock.*
O let there be rejóicing and *Let them say foréver, "God*	glád – ness *ís great,"*	for all *who lóve*	who séek -- you. *your sáv - ing help.*
As for me, wrétched *You are my réscuer,*	ánd poor, *mý help;*	hasten *O LÓRD,*	to mé, O God. *do nót de - lay.*

II

In Gregorian style

Denis Drobinski

♩=170

Choir

God _____ will kill the Shep - herd_____ and the flock will be. scat _____

_____ter'd   And be - fore _____

Solo

_____ the roos - ter crows,   You will de - ny me three times.

The second candle is extinguished

Michelangelo Caravaggio (1571-1610) Denial of St. Peter

4

Psalm 74

Why, O God, have you cást us off for - *Remémber your flock which you claimed long*	é - ver? á - go,	Why does your anger bláze at the sheep of *the tribe you redéemed to be your ówn possession, | this móuntain of Síon where you made*	yóur pas-- - ture? *your dwél-- - ling.*
Turn your stéps to these pláces that are utterly *Your fóes have made uproar in the mídst of your as -*	rú - ined! sém - bly;	The énemy has laid wáste the whole of *they have sét up their émblems*	the hó – ly place. *as tó – kens-there.*
They have wíelded their áxes on high, | as at the entrance to a grove *O Gód, | they have sét your holy place*	óf trees. ón fire;	They have bróken down all the cárvings; | they have strúck together with hatchet *they have rázed and profáned the abode*	and píck-- - ax. *of yóur -- - name.*
They said in their heárts, "We will utterly *We do not see our émblems, nor is there a*	crúsh them; pró - phet;	we will búrn every shríne of *we have no one to téll us how lóng*	God ín the land." *it wíll-- last.*
How lóng, O God, is the énemy *Why, O Lórd, do you hold back*	to scóff? yóur hand?	Is the foe to insúlt your *Why do you kéep your ríght hand hidden*	name for – e - ver? in yóur -- - cloak?
Yet Gód is my king from *It was yóu who divíded the sea by*	tíme past, yóur might,	who bestóws salvátion through *who sháttered the heads of the mon -*	all thé-- land. *sters ín the sea.*
It was yóu who crushed Levía - *It was yóu who opened up spríngs and*	than's heads, tór - rents;	and gave him as fóod to the beasts *it was yóu who dried up ever-flow -*	of thé de - sert. *ing ívy rív -- - ers.*
Yóurs is the day and yóurs is *It was yóu who fixed the bóunds of*	thé night; *thé earth,*	it was yóu who estáblished the *yóu who made bóth summer*	light and the sun. *and wín -- - ter.*
Remember this, O LÓRD: the ene - *Do not give the sóul of your dóve to*	mý scoffed! *thé beasts,*	A sénseless people insúl - *nor forgét the life of your póor ones*	ted yóur -- name! *for – é --- ver.*
Lóok to the cóvenant; each cave in *Do not let the oppréssed be put*	thé land *tó shame;*	is a pláce where violence *let the póor and the néedy*	makes íts -- home. *bless yóur -- name.*
Aríse, O God, and defénd *Do not forget the clámor of*	yóur cause! *yóur foes,*	Remémber how the sénseless revíle *the unceásing uproar of thóse*	you áll the day. *who de -fý you.*

III

In Gregorian style

Denis Drobinski

Solo ♩=170

Fa _____ ther! Fa _____ ther!

6 Men   Solo

Take this cup!   Take this cup!   Take

12

_____ this   cup _____ a - way   from   me! _____

16 Men

Thy   will   not   my   will   be   done _____

The third candle is extinguished

Then is said:

P. Deliver me, my God, from the hand of the wicked.

R. From the clutches of the evildoer and the oppressor.

Caravaggio (1571-1610)
Taking of Christ

The cantor sings the Lamentations

A reading from the Lamentations of the Prophet Jere – <u>mi</u> – ah

[musical notation with measures numbered 1, 2, 3]

1 How lonely sits the city that was full of peo - <u>ple</u>!

How like a widow has she become, she that was great among the <u>na</u> - tions!

She that was a princess among the cities has become a <u>vas</u> - sal.

2 She weeps bitterly in the night, tears on her <u>cheeks</u>;

among all her lovers she has none to com - <u>fort</u> her;

all her friends have dealt treacherously with her, they have become her e – <u>ne</u> - mies.

3 Judah has gone into exile because of affliction and hard servi - <u>tude</u>;

she dwells now among the nations, but finds no rest - <u>ing</u> place;

her pursuers have all overtaken her in the midst of her <u>dis</u> - tress.

4 The roads to Zion mourn, for none come to the appointed <u>feasts</u>;

all her gates are de – <u>so</u> - late,

her priests groan; | her maidens have been dragged away, | and she herself suffers bit – <u>ter</u> -

ly.

5 Her foes have become the head, her enemies pros - <u>per</u>,

because the LORD has made her suffer for the multitude of her trans – <u>gres</u> - sions;

her children have gone away, | captives before <u>the</u> foe.

R. Jerusalem, | Jerusalem, | return to the Lord <u>your</u> God!

Francois Joseph Navez (1787-1869)
Le Massacre Des Innocents

7

After a period of silence, this Responsory is recited:

P. On the Mount of Olives, Jesus prayed to the Father: "Father, if it be possible, let this cup pass from me."

R. The spirit indeed is willing, but the flesh is weak.

P. Watch and pray, that you may not enter into temptation.

R. The spirit indeed is willing, but the flesh is weak.

After a period of silence, the reading continues:

6 From the daughter of Zion has departed all her majes - <u>ty</u>.

Her princes have become like harts that find no <u>pas</u> - ture;

they fled without strength before the pur – <u>su</u> - er.

7 Jerusalem remembers in the days of her affliction and bitterness |

all the precious things that were hers from days of <u>old</u>.

When her people fell into the hand of <u>the</u> foe,

and there was none to help her, the foe gloated over her, mocking at her <u>down</u> - fall.

8 Jerusalem sinned grievously, therefore she became fil - <u>thy</u>;

all who honored her despise her, for they have seen her nak – <u>ed</u> - ness;

yea, she herself groans, and turns her face a - <u>way</u>.

9 Her uncleanness was in her skirts; she took no thought of her <u>doom</u>;

Therefore her fall is terrible, she has no com – <u>for</u> - ter.

"O LORD, behold my affliction, for the enemy has <u>tri</u> - umphed!"

R. Jerusalem, | Jerusalem, | return to the Lord <u>your</u> God!

After a period of silence, this Responsory is recited:

P. My soul is very sorrowful, even to the point of death; remain here, and watch with me. Now you will see the crowd who will surround me;

R. You will flee, and I will go to be offered up for you.

P. Behold, the hour is at hand, and the Son of Man is betrayed into the hands of sinners.

R. You will flee, and I will go to be offered up for you.

After a period of silence, the reading continues:

10 The enemy has stretched out his hands over all her precious things;

Yea, she has seen the nations invade her sanc – tuary,

Those whom Thou hast forbid to enter thy congre – ga - tion.

11 All her people groan as they search for bread;

they trade their treasures for food to revive their strength.

"Look, O LORD, and behold, for I am des - pised."

12 "Is it nothing to you, all you who pass by?

Look and see if there is any sorrow like my sorrow which was brought up - on me,

which the LORD inflicted on the day of his fierce an - ger.

13 "From on high he sent fire; into my bones he made it des - cend;

he spread a net for my feet; he turned me back;

he has left me stunned, faint all the day long.

14 "My transgressions were bound into a yoke; | By his hand they were fastened toge - ther;

They were set upon my neck; he caused my strength to fail;

The Lord gave me into the hand of those whom I cannot with - stand.

R. Jerusalem, | Jerusalem, | return to the Lord your God!

P. Lo, we have seen him without beauty or majesty, with no looks to attract our eyes. He bore our sins and grieved for us, he was wounded for our transgressions,

R. And by his scourging we are healed,

P. Surely he has borne our grief and carried our sorrows.

R. And by his scourging we are healed,

Psalm 63:1-8

O Gód, you are my God; at dáwn I seek you;| for you my soul is *I have cóme befóre you in the*	thírst - ing. *sánc -tuary,*	For you my flésh is pining, | like a drý, weary lánd with - *to behold your stréngth*	out wá -- - ter. *and yóur glo - ry.*
Your loving mércy is better *I will bléss you all*	thán life; *mý life;*	my líps will *in your náme I will lift*	speak yóur -- praise. *up mý -- hands.*
My sóul shall be fílled as with a *When I remémber you upon*	bán - quet; *mý bed,*	with jóyful lips, my mouth *I múse on you through the watches*	shall práise-- you. *of thé -- night.*
For yóu have been *My sóul clings fast*	mý strength; *tó you;*	in the shádow of your wings *your ríght hand*	I ré -- - joice. *up - hólds -- me.*

IV

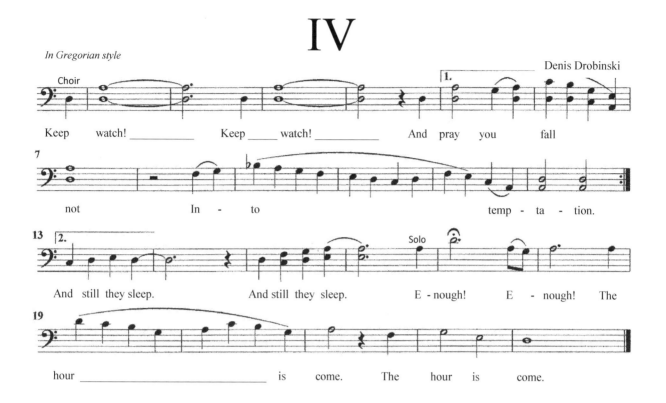

In Gregorian style

Denis Drobinski

Choir

1.

Keep   watch! _____   Keep _____ watch! _____   And   pray   you   fall

7

not   In - to   temp - ta - tion.

13 **2.**

And   still they sleep.   And still they sleep.   E - nough!   E - nough!   The

19

hour _____ is   come.   The   hour   is   come.

The fourth candle is extinguished

Sandro Botticelli (1445-1510) Apostles Sleeping in the Garden

11

Canticle of Hezekiah – Isaiah 38:10-20

I said: In the nóontide of my days I must *I said, I sháll not see the LÓRD in the land of the*	dé - part; *lív - ing;*	I am consígned to the gates of Shéol for the rest *I shall lóok upon mortals no more among the inhábitants*	of mý -- years. *of thé -- world.*
My dwélling is plucked up and remóved from me like a shep - *He cúts me off from*	hérd's tent; *thé loom;*	like a wéaver I have rolled *from dáy to night you bríng me*	up mý -- life; *to án -- end;*
I crý for help until *From dáy to night you bring me to*	mórn - ing; *án end.*	like a líon he bréaks *Like a swállow or a crane I clámor, | I*	all mý -- bones; moan líke a dove.
My eyes are wéary with looking *But what can*	úp - ward. *Í say?*	O Lórd, I am oppréssed; | be my *For he has spóken to me, |and he himself*	se - cúr – i - ty! *has dóne -- it.*
All my sleep *O Lórd, by these things peo -*	hás fled *plé live,*	because of the bítterness *and in áll these is the life of*	of mý -- soul. *my spír -- it.*
Oh, restóre me to health and make *But you have held back my lífe from the pit of des -*	mé live! *trúc - tion,*	Surely it was for my wélfare that I had great *for you have cást all my sins be -*	bit – ter - ness; *hind yóur --back.*
For Sheol cannot thánk you, | death cannot *The líving, the líving, they thánk you , as I do*	práise you; *thís day;*	thóse who go dówn to the Pit cannot hópe for your *the fáthers make known to chíldren your*	faith – fúl -- ness. *faith – fúl -- ness.*
The LÓRD will 	sáve me, 	and we will síng to stringed instruments all the dáys of our life, | at the house	of the -- LORD.

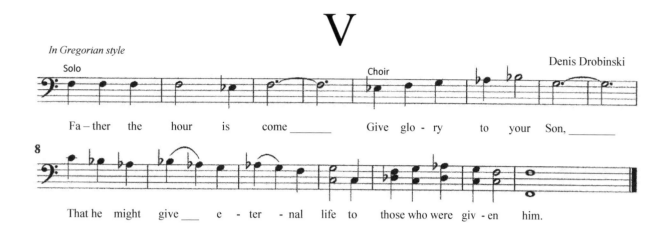

V

In Gregorian style

Denis Drobinski

Fa – ther the hour is come _____ Give glo - ry to your Son, _____

That he might give ___ e - ter - nal life to those who were giv - en him.

The fifth candle is extinguished

Psalm 150

Praise Gód in his ho -	lý place;	práise him in his mighty	fir - má -- ment.
Práise him for his power -	*fúl deeds;*	*práise him for his bound-*	*less grán - -- deur.*
O práise him with sound of	trúm - pet;	práise him with	lute ánd -- -harp.
Práise him with timbrel	*ánd dance;*	*práise him with*	*strings ánd -- -* *pipes.*
O práise him with resounding	cým - bals;	práise him with clashing	of cým -- - bals.
Let éverything that breathes			*praise the -- LORD!*

VI

In Gregorian style

Denis Drobinski

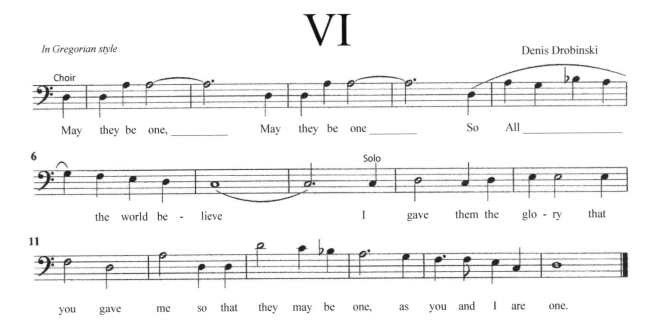

Choir

May they be one, _____ May they be one _____ So All _____

6

the world be - lieve I gave them the glo - ry that

11

you gave me so that they may be one, as you and I are one.

The sixth candle is extinguished

Then is said:

P. My flesh also shall rest in hope:

R. You will not let your Holy One see corruption.

Michelangelo Caravaggio (1571-1610)
Crown of Thorns

Now all other lights except for the single
remaining candle are turned off or turned
down

Canticle of Zecharieh – Luke 1:68-79

"Blessed be the Lórd, the God of Is -	rá - el,	for he has looked fávorably on his péople and	re – déemed-- them.
He has ráised up a mighty sávior	*fór us*	*in the hóuse of his ser -*	*vant Dá -- - vid*
As he spóke through the mouth of his holy próphets from	óf old,	that we would be sáved from our énemies | and from the hánd of all	who háte -- - us.
Thús he has shown the mercy prómised to our	*án - cestors*	*and has remémbered his ho -*	*ly có – ve - nant,*
the oath he swóre to our ancestor	Á - braham:	to gránt us that we, | being réscued from the hands of	our e – ne - mies,
might serve him with -	*óut fear*	*in hóliness and ríghteousness before*	*him áll our days.*
And yóu, my child, will be called the próphet of the	Móst High;	for you will gó on before the Lórd to	pre – páre his ways,
to give knówledge of salvation to his	*péo - ple*	*by the forgíveness*	*of théir -- sins,*
By of the tender mércy of	óur God,	the dáwn on hígh will break	up – ón --- us
to give líght to those who sit in dárkness and in the shádow	*óf death,*	*to gúide our feet into*	*the way óf peace."*

15

VII

In Gregorian style

Denis Drobinski

Choir

Whom _____ do you seek?   Whom _____ do you seek?

Je - sus of Naz - a - reth   Je - sus of

Naz - a - reth   Ah _____ I am He ...

After the singing, the remaining candle is hidden or extinguished, if necessary.

Kneel, if you can, for the following:

P. Christ for our sake became obedient unto death, even death upon a cross; therefore God has highly exalted him and bestowed on him the Name which is above every name.

Psalm 51

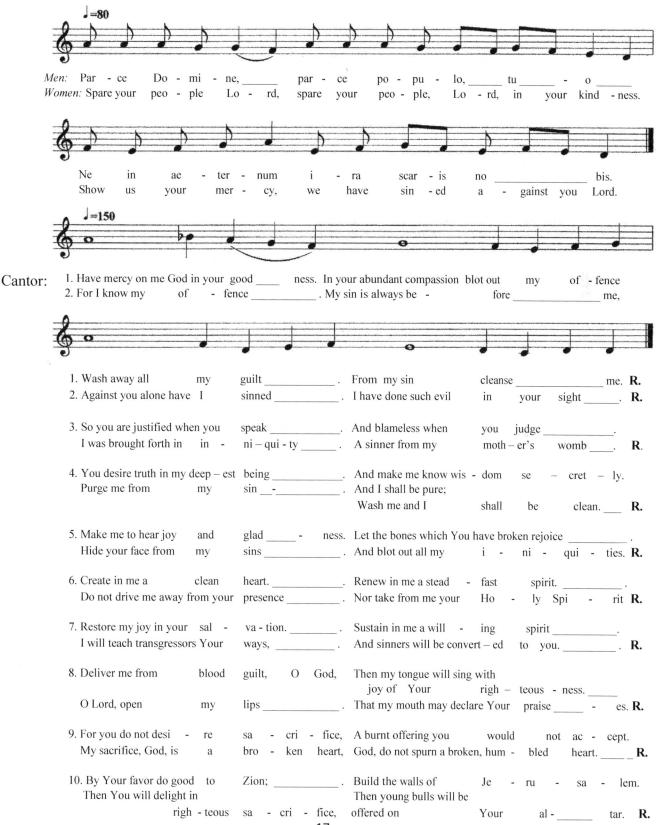

♩=80

Men: Par - ce   Do - mi - ne,_____   par - ce   po - pu - lo,_____ tu_____ - o_____
Women: Spare your peo - ple Lo - rd, spare your peo - ple, Lo - rd, in your kind - ness.

Ne   in   ae - ter - num   i - ra   scar - is   no _____ bis.
Show us your mer - cy, we have sin - ed a - gainst you Lord.

♩=150

Cantor: 1. Have mercy on me God in your good ____ ness. In your abundant compassion blot out my of - fence
2. For I know my of - fence _____ . My sin is always be - fore _____ me,

1. Wash away all my guilt _____ . From my sin cleanse _____ me. **R.**
2. Against you alone have I sinned _____ . I have done such evil in your sight _____ . **R.**

3. So you are justified when you speak _____ . And blameless when you judge _____ .
   I was brought forth in in - ni – qui - ty _____ . A sinner from my moth – er's womb ____ . **R.**

4. You desire truth in my deep – est being _____ . And make me know wis - dom se – cret - ly.
   Purge me from my sin _-_____ . And I shall be pure;
   Wash me and I shall be clean. ____ **R.**

5. Make me to hear joy and glad _____ - ness. Let the bones which You have broken rejoice _____ .
   Hide your face from my sins _____ . And blot out all my i - ni - qui - ties. **R.**

6. Create in me a clean heart. _____ . Renew in me a stead - fast spirit. _____ .
   Do not drive me away from your presence _____ . Nor take from me your Ho - ly Spi - rit **R.**

7. Restore my joy in your sal - va - tion. _____ . Sustain in me a will - ing spirit _____ .
   I will teach transgressors Your ways, _____ . And sinners will be convert – ed to you. _____ . **R.**

8. Deliver me from blood guilt, O God, Then my tongue will sing with
   joy of Your righ – teous - ness. _____
   O Lord, open my lips _____ . That my mouth may declare Your praise _____ - es. **R.**

9. For you do not desi - re sa - cri - fice, A burnt offering you would not ac - cept.
   My sacrifice, God, is a bro - ken heart, God, do not spurn a broken, hum - bled heart. _____ _ **R.**

10. By Your favor do good to Zion; _____ . Build the walls of Je - ru - sa - lem.
    Then You will delight in Then young bulls will be
    righ - teous sa - cri - fice, offered on Your al - _____ tar. **R.**

Then this prayer is said:

P. Almighty God, we pray that you graciously behold this your family, for whom our Lord Jesus Christ was willing to be betrayed, and given into the hands of sinners, and to suffer death upon the cross.

The choir sings from Mark 15:20-39

VIII

In Gregorian style

Denis Drobinski

They mocked him, They stripped him. They took him out to die. They

Singers exit

nailed him to a wood-en cross to die. _____ Ah _____

(Repeat as needed for recessional)

_____ Ah _____

Nothing further is said; but a loud noise is made, the strepitus, symbolizing the convulsion of nature at the crucifixion. The return of the single light symbolizes the Light of Christ which can never be extinguished.

By its light, all depart in silence.

Albrecht Dürer (1471 – 1528)
Crucifixion

SINGING THE PSALMS USING PSALM TONES

Gregorian chant is the central tradition of Western plainchant, a form of monophonic *A Capella* liturgical chant of Western Christianity that accompanied the celebration of Mass and other ritual services. This vast repertory of chants is the oldest music known as it is the first repertory to have been adequately notated in the 10th century. These chants have such a long tradition — more than ten centuries — because they touch depth in one's very soul and spirituality, and attain a marvelous sense of inner peace.

Psalm tones provide melodic formulas for singing the psalms. Gregorian chant with a single line of melody affords the beauty of a rise and fall of a melodic line.

The basic structure of a line of psalmody is as follows:

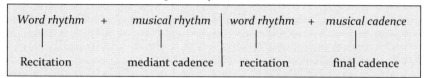

Word rhythm +	*musical rhythm*	*word rhythm* +	*musical cadence*
Recitation	mediant cadence	recitation	final cadence

The psalm tone uses two distinct musical elements. The reciting tone *(recitation)* is sung on one note for a passage of text. The *musical cadences* are a patterns of notes sung according to the laws of musical rhythm. A requirement of recitation is word rhythm with confident forward movement. After the momentum of the recitive, musical rhythm at the cadences conveys a sense of completion and rest.

Although Gregorian Chant written with the original nuems* may require extensive and detailed study of its various subtleties, the psalm-tone chant in this service can be simplified attending to these basic principles:

1. LEGATO - Legato is a term that means "bound together, that is, the singer makes transitions from note to note without intervening silence. The individual notes, therefore, in a musical line are expressed as in natural conversation. Choirs should, then, practice the psalm tones by first reciting the psalms smoothly and not mechanically. Marching through the "singing" of the psalms will repress the soothing and peaceful effect of the chant.

> Legato is one of the characteristics of Gregorian art, which is, above all, prayer... there should therefore be no staccato or hacked out passages, no frequent breaks, ... but always a flowing 'line'; this uninterrupted line follows the melodic line itself, which remains the supreme guide in all that concerns interpretation. Dom Joseph Gajard, O.W.B., *The Solemes Method*

2. ACCENTS – Accents have been placed in the score to improve the undulating characteristic of Gregorian chant, to help the choir stay together and to highlight important concepts of the text.

3. SING RESTFULLY - The chant should be sung in a restful and relaxed pace. No one, either in the choir or in the congregation, should feel agitated by the speed of execution.

4. ENUNCIATE – All of the words, syllables and letters should be enunciated precisely and clearly. Choirs that fail to do this produce a garbled and unintelligible "reading" of the text which completely undermines the purpose of the psalm.

5. PITCH ACCURACY – Singers must stay on pitch or the sound produced is distorted and corrupts the beauty of the presentation.

6. *MORA VOCIS* - It is inconceivable that medieval singers would not have slowed down toward the end of phrases. The *Mora Vocis* or dying away of the voice in Gregorian notation provides direction for this subtle chant style. At the median and final cadences in the psalm tones the last note in the first instance and the last two notes in the second require the singer to slightly lengthen and soften these notes. This greatly enhances the rhythmic element of the chant, checks an inclination to rush through the psalm and provides a peaceful disposition for the chant.

*Neum – A method of musical notation of plainsong used during the middle ages, surviving in transcriptions of Gregorian Chant.

The primary source for the above information is from *A Gregorian Chant Master Class* by Dr. Theodore Marier
© Abbey of Regina Laudis, Bethlehem, CT 06751 2002

Made in the USA
Middletown, DE
01 February 2022

59855314R00015